— epipa —

SUSTAINABLE KNITTING

20 PATTERNS FOR ENVIRONMENTALLY FRIENDLY KNITS

DAVID & CHARLES

www.davidandcharles.com

CONTENTS

PREFACE

As a small child, my parents and grandparents taught me how to live sustainably and protect the environment and its resources in order to continue to live off and with it.

Neither of my grandmothers ever threw anything away if there was even the slightest chance of finding another purpose for it in the house. They either used it again and again, or turned it into something new. How often did I hear the words, "But you can easily do it yourself, child"? And then they showed me how. With ten children between them, my grandmothers had perfected resource-saving life and sustainable housekeeping. They grew their own fruit and vegetables all year round in the garden, which they cooked and preserved. Clothes were passed on, repaired or patched, as long as it was possible and looked good. When they were too far gone even for that, they were reused – repurposed – in many different ways. Fabric was torn into strips and turned into new rugs, made into toys or – if nothing else was possible – used as cleaning rags. We little girls had bright patches from old floral blouses sewn onto our jeans, which we wore for playing.

I could fill another book with the many and inventive examples of how my grandmothers and mother reused and simply reinvented things. I grew up with this wealth of ideas and the joy of thinking 'outside the box', of giving new life to old clothes or objects, and the passion of making things myself.

In this book, we're going to turn old T-shirts, bed linen and tablecloths into our own cotton yarn and restore unravelled yarn from unfinished projects to its former glory. We will craft beautiful, useful and practical things for everyday life; shopping bags and baskets for the larder, place mats and runners for the kitchen, and rugs and accessories for the bathroom.

Finally, I really hope that this book will help you to create lots of lovely projects. For yourself, your home and those who are dear to you. I would be delighted if you would post your finished projects in your InstaStories or feed with the hashtag #sustainableknitting. This will help me to find your channel and share your work with our epipa community. I look forward to it!

And now it only remains for me to wish you lots of happy hours of knitting! Ahead of you are lots of cosy hours of making your own sustainable projects which – just like the ones our grandmothers made – may become much-loved family heirlooms. One thing is certain: something you have made yourself will be a gift that no one ever forgets.

With very best wishes

Yours,

Sascia von epipa

THE BASICS

INTRODUCTION

I am delighted that you have chosen this book. It means that you are interested in living mindfully and sustainably. You don't want to burden the environment unnecessarily, not even when you're knitting – a fabulous decision!

Mindfulness and sustainability are important principles that can be applied to many areas of our lives: from choosing and using less plastic when grocery shopping to sustainable clothing, cosmetics and cleaning products, to our beloved hobby – knitting. It's often the little things that add up to make a big difference. We see it more and more often on the street, in shops and in everyday life: we're opting for reusable bamboo or thermal cups instead of disposable ones, we go shopping with baskets, backpacks or fabric bags so we can avoid the plastic bags in supermarkets and other shops, and we shop at organic and zero waste shops if there are any nearby. These are the things that we can do now.

We can also do a lot to save resources with our hobbies such as knitting, sewing and crocheting. Instead of buying a loveless mass-produced fast-fashion item, we can spend hours sewing, knitting or crocheting a garment, something for the home or a charming little item that not only comes from the heart but also has personality, and can often even become an heirloom.

Good quality fabrics, slow fashion and home-made items can last for decades and bring more love and comfort into everyday life than a modern, statement piece that usually only has to suit current trends for a season. Often it can't do more than that anyway, and will then have to be disposed of because of its poor quality. We know that, and that's why we like to make things by hand.

In this book, I have put together a collection of everyday items for you that you can easily make yourself. As always with my projects, I have tried to leave as much room for manoeuvre as possible in the design, the possible variations and the yarns used. With regard to rugs, baskets, place mats, and table runners, you can rummage through your wardrobe and cupboard or scour flea markets and charity shops for beautiful fabrics. They can all be reused for new projects that will make your home more beautiful.

In this section, you will find a lot of interesting information on the topic of sustainability, and what to remember when buying yarn in a fair, controlled, organic, resource-saving manner.

MINDFUL AND SUSTAINABLE IN THE YARN SHOP

What to do with scraps and forgotten yarn? When we look at our own personal yarn stash, despite careful planning and mindful purchasing behaviours, we will undoubtedly find a few balls or UFOs (unfinished objects) that have been forgotten. Therefore, we have scraps that we haven't used for a long time or won't use anymore, and we can use these up in a variety of ways.

Some yarns we buy because they are so beautiful and we simply couldn't resist them. In our mind, we have already hatched a little plan of what we could use them for, so we bought them. In most cases, they are indeed used for lovely projects. However, I have to say that I haven't used up every single ball of yarn in my home.Knitting is a creative process, and the time and the mood all have to be right for the flow of the project. It's very rare that I stick strictly to a pattern, and I don't actually know anyone who does that unless they are knitting to order. But even then you are offering products that are also fun if you're doing piece-work.

So it's more than possible that the odd ball or two may spend a while in the cupboard and ultimately not really be used for anything, perhaps because the colour or the pattern or the structure of the yarn are a bit outdated. It's also possible that the yarn may still be really lovely, but we now can't use it for what we were originally going to use it for because the recipient's taste has changed, or because a little one has grown too big for the size we had in mind and now there's not enough yarn. If we're unlucky, it might no longer be possible to buy enough of the same yarn for the next size.

Whatever the reasons, most of us have scraps and yarns that we have forgotten about, but it's too much of a shame to get rid of it (and, of course, this would not be a sustainable thing to do). Therefore, we need to find creative ways of using it.

We usually know exactly what to do with pretty scraps: we use these yarns to knit things in lots of different colours, little accessories or useful items. The instructions for these can often be found on the internet or in my books.

UFOs are unpicked, rewound and the yarn reused. Later in this section (see Relaxing Frogged Yarn) I will tell you how to treat unpicked yarn so it looks like new again.

YARNS FROM ANIMALS

No two yarns are the same. We differentiate between wool that is mostly of animal origin, synthetic and plant fibres, and silk. Different yarns can be used for various projects.

WOOL

Clothing has been made from new wool for hundreds of years, and is our first choice when we start thinking about knitting something warm.

It is believed that the mouflon, the ancestor of our present-day domestic sheep, was first domesticated around 10,000 BC. Originally kept as a source of meat, man soon discovered the extraordinary qualities of the animals' fur. Wool provides protection against the heat, cold, wind and rain. However, the wool fibres of the early animals no longer meet the current standard, which is the result of centuries of breeding.

The origins of wool as we know it first began in the Near East. Several centuries and countless continents and cultures later, England and Spain were for a long time the only exporters of the fine wool. Merino wool in particular (named after Beri-Merines), brought from Morocco to Spain by the Moors in the 8th century, was highly sought after and quite literally worth its weight in gold. So much so, in fact, that breeding the animals was banned on pain of death. It was not until the 18th century that the monopoly was dissolved and the animals spread all over Europe.

Do a little research, and you will find plenty of information on the topic of organically farmed pure new wool, which is committed to environmental protection and animal welfare.

SILK

The idea of using silk for manufacturing textiles originated in China, and was mentioned in myths and legends around 3000 BC. Later it was transported to Europe via the Silk Route as an important commodity. According to PETA, in addition to China, Japan, India and Uzbekistan are the largest producers of silk. Like wool, silk is also of animal origin.

Silk is the only naturally occurring continuous fibre, and is obtained from the cocoon of the silkworm, the larva of the silk moth. The caterpillars pupate and lay the coveted protein thread around themselves about 300,000 times until a cocoon is formed. In order to be able to harvest the silk thread as a whole, the cocoons are boiled or exposed to hot steam before the butterfly hatches. This prevents the thread from breaking into individual parts during hatching and reducing the quality of the silk. Silk from intact cocoons is known as breeding silk, mulberry silk or reel silk (silk purified from the silk gum). Approximately 1kg of raw material is required for 250g of silk thread. This equates to about 3,000 cocoons.

The cocoon is unwound by hand, cleaned, reeled and undergoes further production processes until smooth and white. It can be turned into a variety of silk fabrics.

However, there are also other ways and means of making silk. Wild silk, tussah silk or bourette silk are obtained from cocoons and residues that are not processed until the silk moth has hatched. Due to the texture, the fibres are shorter and cannot be reeled, so they have to be thickened at the breakpoints when weaving, which results in the characteristic irregular surface of the textiles with tiny knots, or nodules.

Bourette silk cannot be completely cleaned of silk gum, and is not really very interesting to the fashion industry because of its coarse, linen-like structure. Silk gum, however, also known as silk bast, is said to have anti-inflammatory properties. Bourette silk is therefore often used in the production of baby nappies and breast pads because of its high proportion of silk gum.

THE BASICS

PLANT FIBRES

While vegan alternatives have long been present in the kitchen and are still very much on trend, new materials are now also appearing in the hobby sector that are produced purely from plant-based materials, excluding animal components.

Cotton can be found in any well-stocked yarn shop. Tencel and bamboo viscose, on the other hand, are still among the more exotic vegan yarns. We can change this with our buying behaviour – after all, demand determines supply. Here too, it is important to consider the product in its entirety. Just because a yarn is advertised as vegan doesn't necessarily mean that the topic of sustainability has been considered at every single step of its production. Or that the synthetic fibre is really of plant origin. Polyester is also vegan, but is usually based on crude oil. This is difficult to break down and releases microplastics into the water with every wash.

To give you a small overview of the different plant fibres and their special features, here are the main facts and some specific tips on yarns.

"Be the change you want to see in the world."

Mahatma Gandhi

COTTON

The classic when it comes to vegan yarn. This natural fibre is extremely hard-wearing, and therefore long-lasting. Its soft structure means it is skin-friendly, and ideal for allergy-sufferers. Unlike synthetic yarn, cotton is biodegradable because it consists mainly of cellulose. However, do look out for organic qualities. Although pesticides are often used in conventional cotton production, organically cultivated cotton is free from chemical agents thanks to crop rotations. This means that other plants are grown in the same field between two cotton seeds. Pests that specialise in cotton are unable to multiply to the same extent. Mixed cultivation also protects the cotton plants against less specialised pests because they prefer to attack the other plants. Even the tremendous amount of water that is required in cotton production is managed better in this type of growing because the soil dries out more slowly. Turkey is the biggest exporter of organic cotton. However, India and Egypt are also considered to be important locations in the production of organic cotton.

YARN TIP FOR COTTON

The 'Linea Pura' collection by Lana Grossa includes ORGANICO. This consists of 100 percent sustainably grown organic cotton, and is available in 42 colours. It is also certified with the globally recognised GOTS seal (p. 21). This basic yarn is excellent, for instance, for make-up remover pads (p. 105), but also for kitchen towels (p. 65) and, of course, for clothing.

YARN TIP FOR PIMA COTTON

The yarn 'Cumbria' by Pascuali contains 60 percent Pima cotton. The remaining 40 percent is viscose, which is made from bamboo pulp and is imported from China. The blend of these two fibres feels similar to a merino silk yarn. This composition also reduces water consumption during production, which is much higher for cotton than viscose. The vegan product is processed entirely in Peru, and follows a sustainable concept from fibre production to packaging material; for instance, the sludge that is produced during the washing of the fibres is used again as fertiliser for the fields. The yarn is available in 18 colours.

PIMA COTTON

This variety differs from conventional cotton with regards to fibre length and thickness. Whilst conventional cotton fibres are usually between 13 and 19 millimetres long, Pima cotton's fibres have a length of around 35 millimetres. It is grown in Peru, mainly in the northern coastal valleys where the climate, being close to the equator, is perfect for the plants. Something else that is special about it is that it is only picked by hand. This makes production more environmentally-friendly with no risk of the fibres breaking. Pima cotton is considered a vegan alternative to silk because it is almost as soft and temperature-regulating as its animal counterpart. Its anti-allergenic properties make it particularly suitable for babies and people with sensitive and delicate skin.

LINEN

Linen is obtained from the stems of the flax plant and, along with cotton, hemp, wool and silk, is one of the natural fibres used in the production of textiles. We distinguish between half linen and linen. Half linen consists of cotton with a minimum flax content of 40 percent, while pure linen is made of 100 percent flax. In contrast to other bast fibres, linen fibres are easy to divide and finely spin, which makes it ideal for the production of underwear (linens) and clothing.

Since the linen fibre is smooth and linen fabric contains little air, linen is lint-free and not very susceptible to dirt and bacteria. The fibre is naturally antiseptic, antistatic and dirt-repellent. Linen can absorb up to 35 percent humidity, which it quickly releases back into the ambient air. This means it is cooling, but also dry and warm.

HEMP

Hemp is extremely popular as a fast-growing raw material for its many different uses. In addition to hemp pulp and hemp paper, hemp textiles are the most important product made of hemp fibres. The oldest known findings of textiles made from hemp fibres come from China, and date back to about 2800 BC. Until the 19th century, hemp fibres were among the most important raw materials for the European textile industry, along with flax, nettles and wool. Clothing made from hemp also absorbs around 30 percent of moisture, which makes it very pleasant to wear.

No herbicides are required when growing hemp, as the plant completely shades the soil after just a few days, preventing weeds from growing. It is also highly resistant to pests and very easy to care for, so no chemical agents are required in its cultivation.

RECYCLED YARNS

In Germany alone, households generate around 1.35 million tonnes of worn clothing every year. As a representative survey by Greenpeace has shown, one in five garments is almost never worn before it is retired. These are grim figures. Apart from rethinking our buying habits, we can also do something else in this area. We can make yarn from old T-shirts and cotton fabrics ourselves, and turn them into something new. So we can re-use and re-purpose once-loved favourites, bed linen and clothes that we no longer wear – perhaps even making them better and more durable than before.

The yarn industry has also given some thought to the subject of recycling, and many manufacturers now offer recycled yarns, some of which are 100% recycled and some that do have new fibres added but neverthless contain a high proportion of recycled materials. They process discarded textiles and production waste from the fashion industry, which also helps to save further resources and reduces the burden on the environment.

CASHMERE

Rico Design uses surpluses from the production of cashmere clothing for its 'Essential Cashmere Recycled dk' yarn. The material is carefully brushed to restore it to its original non-woven form. It is then spun again, and a cosy, snuggly cashmere yarn is created - one that is ideal for winter accessories such as scarves and headbands, but also for jumpers and cardigans.

DENIM

Old jeans, on the other hand, are recycled by the manufacturers of the Spanish DIY brand We Are Knitters. Instead of ending up in landfill, old denim garments are broken down into their individual fibres and spun into a strong new yarn for its 'Recycled Yarn'. Its eye-catching structure gives the garments a rustic look, and is ideal for springtime sweaters and tops. There are six colours to choose from: dark blue, sky blue, wine red, natural white, marbled pink and grey.

COTTON

Reva yarn by the company ggh consists of 95 percent recycled cotton. The manufacturer also opted for the used look in the design – all 14 colours are lightly mottled. This effect gives the yarn a special denim look. The yarn is particularly suitable for summer knitting projects, such as delicate scarves, tops and lightweight cardigans.

Another example is The Tape by We Are Knitters, which is mostly made of recycled T-shirt fibres and dyed with safe dyes.

YARN INNOVATIONS

In the search for environmentally sound alternatives, industries and researchers are constantly striving to find new ways to meet the demands of consumers whilst at the same time protecting the environment. Yarns made from bamboo, corn starch, and wood fibres may sound reassuringly sustainable at first (and probably are thanks to the natural raw materials) but a certain amount of toxic chemicals will nonetheless be required during the production process.

BAMBOO, WOOD, TENCEL

The IVN (International Association of Natural Textile Industry) does not recognise viscose made from the above raw materials as harmless. The difference between viscose and natural fibres is that viscose can only be spun after complex chemical conversion processes. The intensive chemical treatment that must be applied produces a considerable amount of harmful intermediate products.

CORN YARN

Technically, polylactide (PLA), corn yarn is made from corn starch. What the yarn label does not tell us: polylactides are synthetic polymers and belong to the polyester family. PLAs may biodegrade in just a few months, but only under certain environmental conditions, such as those that are only found in industrial composting plants. In nature, PLA decomposes much more slowly, and is therefore also called an organic microplastic.

SOY SILK

Yarn made of soy fibres should also be regarded with caution. Although it is advertised that the fibre used in its production comes from a by-product of tofu processing, the cultivation of soya is not without criticism. The cultivation of the soybean for the animal feed industry, which uses 80 percent of the soybean harvest, has been criticised. Soya cultivation is responsible for monocultures and the expulsion of indigenous peoples from their homelands. In fact, only a small proportion – 20 percent – of the total soya cultivation is used for food, so soy silk cannot necessarily be considered harmless.

We should not vilify innovations from the outset. However, it's advisable for all of us to have a healthy mistrust and do some research when we come across a much-praised innovation accompanied with shiny promises.

STANDARDS AND CERTIFICATIONS

Various seals can provide information on the production conditions used for a yarn. Sadly though, many of the smaller producers cannot afford expensive certifications. Asking a manufacturer directly about its company's ethical principles is a good way of finding out whether the yarn was appropriately husbanded and its production environmentally friendly.

For sheep wool, look for products with organic certification if you want to buy yarn for which no animals have suffered. Organic certification varies depending on the body but it generally ensures that animals are kept in an appropriate way according to the needs of their species; this means no fattening aids are used, the animals have plenty of space in pesticide- and insecticide-free pastures, they are allowed to reproduce naturally, and they are fed specially controlled food.

Organic certification for vegetable fibres varies depending on the certification body, but generally stipulates that plants must not be treated with pesticides or be genetically modified. Furthermore, harvesting must be done by hand and weeds must not be treated with herbicides. Strict rules also apply to further processing (for instance, no harmful chemicals can be used).

In order to obtain the GOTS seal (Global Organic Textile Standards), 70 percent of fibres in the product must be certified organically farmed. If the term 'organic' is to be used, it has to be as much as 95 percent. Organic farming also applies in the case of fibres of animal origin. In addition, chlorine bleaching must not be used in further processing. Furthermore the GOTS seal is also subject to compliance with social standards. These include the payment of minimum wages, health and safety protection in the workplace, and the prohibition of child and forced labour.

The OEKO TEX® product labels are probably among the best-known certifications. For instance, if yarn bears the MADE IN GREEN by OEKO TEX® seal, then it has undergone extensive testing for harmful substances. National and international limits and directives must be observed in order to rule out any health hazards. In addition to the successful testing for pollutants as per STANDARD 100, MADE IN GREEN also calls for compliance with environmentally-friendly production technologies and socially responsible working conditions.

MAKE YOUR OWN
T-SHIRT YARN

Skills: Beginner, very easy

I always like to use old clothes, tablecloths and duvet covers, retired or from a flea market, and breathe new life into them. With just a few snips, you can turn T-shirts into yarn for little baskets and mats.

Materials
• Used, stretch cotton T-shirt
• Scissors

INSTRUCTIONS

Place the T-shirt on a smooth surface. Cut in a straight line across the front and back under the armpits, cutting through both layers at the same time. Cut off the bottom hem of the T-shirt. This will leave you with a loop.

Place the loop on your work surface with the open edges at the sides and the original side seams at the top and bottom.

Now fold the nearest side seam up towards the further one. Place these two edges so that the lower one is protruding by about 2cm (1in).

Starting at the bottom fold, cut up in a straight line 2cm (1in) from the open edge until you have cut through the first top side seam. Leave the other side seam intact so that the yarn can be wound in a single piece later on. Place a parallel cut at the side and continue in a width of approx. 2cm (1in) until you have cut up the whole T-shirt.

Now unfold the T-shirt on the remaining intact side, and cut this seam into strips working diagonally from right to left. The first and last cuts cut through the T-shirt to create the start and end of the long strip.

The cut T-shirt should now consist of one long piece of fabric. Gently stretch the fabric lengthwise until the sides of the strip roll in.

MAKE YOUR OWN
COTTON TAPE YARN

Skills: Beginner, very easy

Beautiful yarns can be made from old woven cotton fabrics such as tablecloths, bed linen or curtains. Torn into strips, rolled into balls and knitted up, they can be used to make lovely rugs, runners and place mats. Plain fabrics give your knitted item a calm appearance, while patterned fabrics produce wonderful marls.

Materials
- Woven cotton fabric, e.g. duvet cover
- Scissors

INSTRUCTIONS

Cut the cover along all the seams. This will leave you with two large pieces (large rectangles).

The fabric strips should be no narrower than 1.5cm (⅝in) and no wider than 2.5cm (1in). If they are too narrow, there is a risk of the fabric strip tearing; if they are too wide you will find it almost impossible to knit with them.

For the yarn strips, tear the fabric into strips starting at the narrow edge of the cover. Use scissors and starting at the edge, snip into the fabric at 1.5cm (⅝in) and tear it lengthwise from here. High-quality woven fabrics tear neatly along the grain to the end of the length of fabric.

When you have torn the cover into strips, tie the ends together **(1 & 2)** and wind up into a ball of yarn.

The protruding ends and rough edges will create a slightly rustic appearance.

For an even surface: sew the strips together with needle and thread and twist them slightly while winding them to conceal the torn edges.

RELAXING
FROGGED YARN

Skills: Beginner, very easy

Of course, from time to time you may find that a project hasn't turned out as well as you wanted, or perhaps you don't like it or just don't finish it. It can then be difficult to use the unpicked yarn (frogged yarn) for new projects, because it is uneven where it was knitted. But with a little patience, you can easily relax frogged yarn and use it for new projects.

Materials
- Unfinished project (UFO)
- or unpicked yarn (frogged yarn)
- String or scraps of yarn

INSTRUCTIONS

Unpick the UFO and wind the yarn into a skein on a yarn swift. If you don't have a swift, you can also use a straight chair back or even your own forearm to wind the yarn around, between your hand to your elbow. It doesn't matter how long the skein is. All that matters is that you have one or, depending on the size of the UFO, several skeins of yarn in front of you.

When all the skeins have been wound, use some scraps or string to secure the individual strands in the skein. This prevents them from knotting. Tie the wool together loosely in three or four places with the string.

Immerse the yarn in the sink or a bucket of water until it is soaked. Do not stir! Lift out the yarn. Gently squeeze out the excess water – do not wring! Allow a single skein to drain over the sink. If you have several skeins, it is better to hang them in the shower or over the bath. You can collect the dripping water in buckets and use it e.g. to water the flowers. The yarn is best left to dry overnight. Do not hang in sunlight, and do not place on a heater as this will damage the fibres. Their own weight will pull the strands down so they dry straight. If the yarn is very twisted, you might want to put weights on it.

THE COLOURS

Most of the yarns that we see in shops are chemically dyed. Here, too,
there are differences in the sustainability of dyeing processes.

I can really only skim the surface of the topic of self-dyeing in this book, and describe only one of the many ways of doing it. This subject is so varied that it fills entire books, and it certainly goes beyond the scope of this one. If you would like to go into the subject more deeply, then a little research on the internet will yield a lot of information. Be it the dyeing of yarn with food or vegetable dyes, dyeing in a saucepan or the oven, using vinegar or alum as a mordant, recipes for dyes and sources of natural dyes and colourants. I would generally encourage anyone to simply try it because the dyeing process is always exciting. Choosing the right yarn and the dyes; mordants; stirring and mixing the colours, the actual process of dyeing, and the moment of truth. You won't always get the expected results straight away –the actual colouration can vary greatly from the set idea, especially at the beginning. No two dye baths are the same, but to me that is the particular charm of DIY dyeing.

Ready-mixed dyes are more expensive than plant substances, such as onion peel or avocado stones, but less sensitive in the durability of the colouring. The results are also easier to reproduce, and therefore a better choice for beginners. They are ideal for achieving effects, mixtures or colour gradations. Retailers offer countless options as well as ready-made kits for self-dyeing.

If you want to experiment with plant substances yourself, remember that acid-based colourings such as food or acid dyes are best absorbed by purely animal fibres. Depending on their composition and any auxiliary fibres, vegetable yarns do not always absorb the colours completely or evenly. This can lead to beautiful effects such as marls, but also to disappointment if the results do not match your expectations. So it is best to take a close look at the manufacturer's instructions and recommendations concerning natural dyes, to use yarns with a wool content of at least 70 percent to start with, and simply to be open to the natural process. If the first colourings are successful, then you can carry on experimenting on this basis; the possibilities are endless. In any case, I always recommend keeping a colouring journal and accurately recording mixing ratios, results and impressions. Over time, you will have a personal recipe book for colour blends, yarn qualities and dye baths.

UNDYED YARN AND DYES

Undyed yarn and dyes for dyeing them yourself are available from various small and large shops on the internet. It is always important that the manufacturers should have a transparent corporate philosophy or certifications confirming compliance with animal welfare and environmental standards.

The website of the company Schmusewolle.de, for example, offers a wide range of dyed and undyed yarns for dyeing yourself. The company's philosophy is based on a particularly environmentally-friendly production chain. For example, the manufacturers only source their German wool from selected shepherds, stating that they rely on particularly caring husbandry, animal-friendly shearing, and environmentally-friendly dyeing methods for their coloured wools. Yarns from Schmusewolle.de are 100 percent mulesing-free. Dyes and equipment for DIY dyeing are also available from their internet shop.

Ready-made dyeing kits with all the tools for the process are available from various sources including myboshi. In addition to alum salt as a mordant, the kit also includes the prepared dyeing plant. Even the yarn is included. With six colours in total, myboshi offers a good basic palette for initial dyeing experiments such as a light yellow (barberry), olive (birch), violet-grey (logwood), black-grey (pomegranate), pink-red (madder root) and yellow-orange (turmeric).

DYEING YARN WITH FOOD COLOURINGS

Skills: Beginner, very easy

Materials
- 100% cotton or wool yarn in a skein, 50g (2oz)
- Powder food dyes
- Vinegar
- Baking tray
- Syringe, pipette or spoon

INSTRUCTIONS

Yarn has to be prepared for dyeing. This will loosen the fibres, causing them to separate like the individual layers in a pinecone, so they absorb the dye better and it lasts longer. Prepare the bath with warm water and plenty of vinegar. I use 250ml (8 floz) vinegar to about 1 litre (2 pints) of water. Make sure that the yarn is completely submerged. Air bubbles mean dry areas that take on no colour, or almost no colour. Ideally, soak the yarn in the bath overnight.

After soaking, carefully squeeze out the yarn with your hands – do not wring! Then leave to drip, but not for too long because the yarn must still be damp for dyeing.

Now prepare the dye. Small bowls or cups made of ceramic are best for this purpose. It's easier to add the dyes with a syringe or pipette, but a spoon will also do the job.

Put the powder in the little bowls, stir with a little vinegar water and test the dye on kitchen paper first until you have the colour you want. Less water and lots of dye = strong shades. More water and less dye = softer shades. There are no fixed recipes here; you can do as you please and dye to suit your personal taste. I prefer pastel shades. The colours can be applied to the yarn pure or mixed together first, which allows a wider range of colour tones.

To prepare for dyeing, place the damp yarn on a baking tray lined with baking paper.

For monochrome yarn, the damp skein can be placed in a dye bath with warm water until the dye has been absorbed. For marls, apply the dye directly to the yarn with the syringe, pipette or a spoon. For colour gradated yarn, apply several colours to the yarn at intervals. Apply very little colour at first, just to be on the safe side, as the damp yarn will absorb it inside the strand, so the colour will run (as when you hold a handkerchief in a little water). This property of the yarn is useful when you want a smooth gradient from colour to white or colour gradients. For my colours and gentle gradients, I deliberately contrasted the individual colours with a little white.

When you have finished applying the colour, place the baking tray with the yarn in the oven (75° fan) for about 45-60 minutes to set it.

Then rinse out the fixed, dyed yarn under lukewarm water. Do not wring! Rubbing and heat will cause the yarn to felt. Gentle squeezing is enough. The dyed yarn is ready when the water runs clear.

Spread the yarn out on an old towel to dry, but avoid direct sunlight.

YARN

I used natural white yarn, but you can also dye grey, beige, or already-dyed yarn (as long as you are starting with a light colour).

CARE

I wash my dyed yarn normally on the wool programme of my washing machine. The colours are preserved. If you're not sure about this, you can wash it by hand. The beauty of dyeing with food colours: it's quick, easy, and can be done by children. You can use utensils that you already have in the kitchen or that are not expensive to purchase.

DYEING WITH NATURAL MATERIALS

Dyeing with food colours has the advantages of being quick and the colours are mixed without much effort. It's also ideal for those first attempts at dyeing. But if you want to immerse yourself more intensively in the fascinating world of dyeing yarn and fabric, you will find plenty of excellent information and literature on the subject of dyeing with plants or fruits from nature on the internet. Just try it!

SUSTAINABLE CARE

Here are a few tips to help ensure you enjoy your
knitted items for a long time to come.

As a general rule, items hand-knitted in pure wool do not need to be washed very often. As wool is antibacterial, unpleasant smells do not tend to last long, and often items only need to be hung in fresh air overnight. Due to the natural layer of lanolin, sheep's wool fat, wool is also water- and dirt-repellent. As soon as the morning dew has dried, the wool can simply be shaken a little or the relevant area rubbed gently with a cotton cloth.

But not all the wool in the shops still contains lanolin. In fact, it needs to be removed if the wool is to be dyed so that the colours can settle in the fibres. Industrially dyed yarns contain hardly any lanolin, and are more likely to get dirty. A lanolin treatment can help here. Pure undyed natural wool feels a little greasy and has a characteristic smell. As this layer reduces with every wash, we recommend treating garments from time to time with special lanolin detergents.

Garments that are worn next to the skin such as undershirts should not be treated with lanolin, otherwise the fibres will lose wool's typical ability to absorb moisture without feeling wet. These garments will keep the body warm and dry. However, jumpers, hats or wool jackets that are supposed to protect the wearer against bad weather should be washed with lanolin since they are intended to repel dirt and moisture rather than absorb it. Well-stocked organic shops will contain a good selection of organic detergents, lanolin care products, and environmentally-friendly alternatives that will reduce wastewater pollution.

Anyone wanting sustainable wool should note that easy-wash wool with the superwash finish is coated with a thin, smooth layer of plastic during production. This treatment prevents the scaly layer of the wool fibres from spreading during washing and thus from felting. Superwash yarns are therefore strictly speaking synthetic fibres with natural fibre cores, which are less likely to felt, and can also be machine washed up to a certain temperature.

Cotton and recycled yarns are usually even easier to care for than wool. Before a yarn comes onto the market, the manufacturers test them in a wide variety of situations, including care and laundering. It is therefore advisable to check the label, whether animal or vegetable fibre, and follow the manufacturer's instructions. It usually provides information on how to wash and at what temperature, as well as on how to dry or iron.

The numbers in this symbol represent the maximum washing temperature to be set.

 Hand wash only.

 The bar stands for delicate wash. One bar means a reduced spin speed. Two bars means delicate wash.

 Do not wash.

 Clean with perchlorethylene, hydrocarbon, R113 or R11 solution (dry clean by a specialist company).

 Clean with R113 and hydrocarbon solutions (also by a specialist company}.

 Do not dry clean.

 Do not bleach.

OTHER

 Do not wring.

 Dry flat. Do not hang the wet garment up.

DRYING

 May be ironed, but note the temperature that is to be set (shown as 1–3 dots).

 Do not iron with steam.

 Do not iron.

 Do not tumble dry.

OTHER CARE INSTRUCTIONS

- **Spot treat small marks or stains**
- **Use the wool wash programme if the machine has one**
- **If hand washing, do not scrub, and do not wring out the water, but squeeze gently instead**

KNITTING TECHNIQUES

From casting on to sewing in ends, this is where you'll find all the main techniques you need to make the projects in this book.

LONG TAIL CAST ON

First make a slip knot and thread it over your needle. The end of the yarn should be about 3 times as long as your cast on piece will be – a little more if your yarn is thick, a little less if it is thinner.

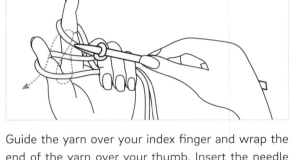

Guide the yarn over your index finger and wrap the end of the yarn over your thumb. Insert the needle under the thread on your left thumb, then over the yarn on your left index finger and pull it towards you through the two thumb lengths as a loop.

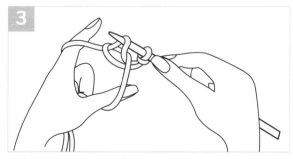

Tighten the new stitch on the needle, and wrap the lengths of yarn around your thumb and index finger again. Repeat steps 2 and 3.

KNIT STITCH

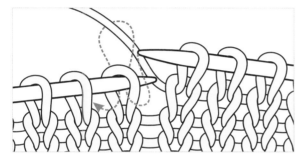

For a knit stitch, insert the needle from the front into the next stitch on the left needle. Then take up the yarn from above and draw through the stitch. The new stitch will be on the right needle; allow the original stitch to slide from the left needle.

Check: The new stitch will be on the needle with the knit side at the front and the purl side at the back.

PURL STITCH

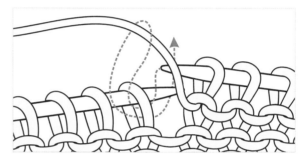

For a purl stitch, insert the needle from the back into the next stitch on the left needle. Then take up the yarn from above and draw through the stitch. The new stitch will be on the right needle; allow the original stitch to slide from the left needle.

Check: The new stitch will be on the needle with the purl side at the front and the knit side at the back.

JOINING YARNS

If you are knitting in rounds, try to join the new yarn at a point where it won't be too obvious when you are wearing the finished garment. If you only want to knit a few rows in the new colour, you can run the other thread up the inside of the garment without having to start all over again whenever you change colours.

STARTING A NEW YARN

If you have finished a ball of wool or want to change colours, be sure that the ends are at least 10cm (4in) long to make it easier to sew them in later on.

Leave the ends hanging and sew them in later
Join the new yarn to the current one with a loose knot. Slide this knot to the beginning of the row, and now continue knitting with the new yarn. You'll untie the knot later on and sew both ends into the edge of the garment (see fig.1).

There will be no edges if you are knitting in rounds. In this case, change the yarns in a spot where it won't be too obvious later on.

T I P

There are various ways of finding out whether the amount of wool in the current ball is enough for another row. Place the item down flat and run the remaining length of yarn four times from the beginning to the end of the row you want to knit. If you are able to do this, you should have enough yarn left for one more row. Remember, though, that more intricate patterns may well use more yarn. Alternative: Tie a knot (not too tightly! You want to be able to untie it again) in the middle of the remaining length of yarn and knit a row. If you haven't reached the knot by the time you get to the end of the row, you can safely knit another row. Otherwise start a new ball of yarn now.

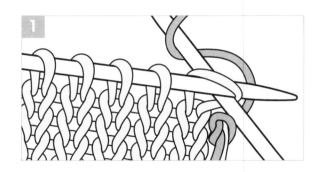

CHANGING COLOURS IN ROUNDS

When changing colours in rounds, unsightly colour 'steps' can be created when you change rounds. You can prevent these by doing the following.

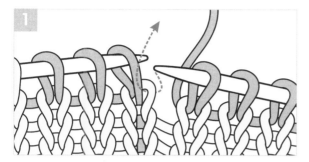

Knit the first round in the new colour.

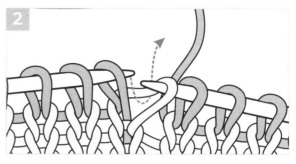

At the beginning of the second round, lift the stitch that is below the first stitch up on to the left needle …

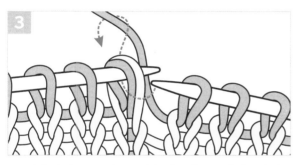

…and knit it together with the first stitch of the second round.

NOTE

If you are changing colours in rounds, you can carry the unused yarn at the back of the item. Cross the lengths of yarn every round to prevent large loops on the back.

SLIP ONE STITCH KNITWISE

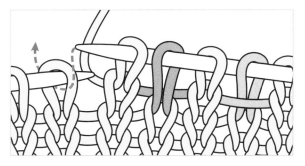

Slip one stitch as if to knit by inserting the needle in the stitch as if to knit, but moving it on to the right needle without knitting it. The light and dark green stitches were both slipped, once with the yarn at the front and then with the yarn at the back. You can tell that the stitches were slipped as if to knit by the leading edge of the stitch being behind the needle.

SLIP ONE STITCH PURLWISE

Slip one stitch as if to purl by inserting the needle in the stitch as if to purl, but moving it on to the right needle without knitting it. Here too, the light and dark green stitches were slipped with the yarn in front and behind the stitch. You can tell that the stitches were slipped as if to purl by the leading edge of the stitch being in front of the needle.

YARN OVER

For yarn-over, place the yarn over the right needle before finishing the next stitch.
Yarn-overs are used for lacy patterns and to increase stitches.

BETWEEN TWO KNIT STITCHES

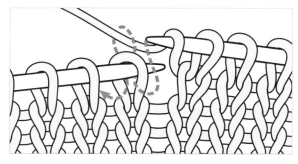

Place the yarn from the front over the right needle and finish the next knit stitch as normal.

KNIT FRONT AND BACK - INCREASE

Insert the right needle in the next stitch as if to knit...

... and draw the yarn through.

Do not allow the stitch to slide from the needle yet...

...but instead knit into it again once twisted (that is, through the back of the stitch).

Let the stitch slide off the left needle.

KNIT 2 TOGETHER – DECREASE

This decrease looks as if it is tilting to the right in the knitted piece.

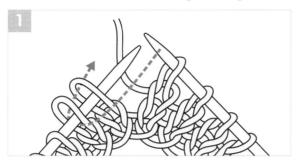

Guide the needle from left to right first through the next stitch but one, then through the next stitch on the left needle.

Draw the yarn through as for a knit stitch.

Allow both stitches to slide from the left needle. You can, of course, knit three or more stitches together in the same way.

BASIC CAST-OFF

The easiest way to cast off is the basic cast-off. This method is the same for knit and purl stitches.

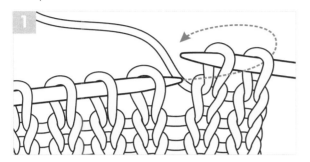

Knit the first two stitches normally, then insert the left needle from the left into the first knitted stitch.

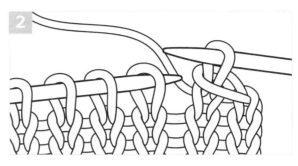

Pull this stitch over the one to the left of it, then allow the stitch to slide from the needle. And you have cast off a stitch. Knit the next stitch as normal, and again cast off the stitch to the right of it.

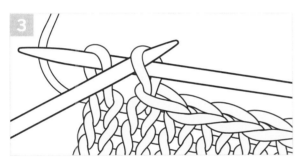

Repeat to the end of the row. Then draw the end of the yarn through the last stitch, leaving a length of at least 10cm (4in) for when you sew it in later.

NOTE

Use the same principle to cast off purl stitches or in a pattern. The stitches are always worked as they appear, knit the knit stitches, purl the purl stitches.

SEWING IN ENDS

You need to sew in all the ends left by changing colours or balls when you have finished your knitting. This is much easier if you take care to leave the ends nice and long – at least 10cm (4in) – when you cast on, cast off or change colours.

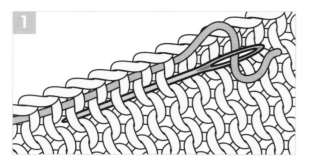

Ideally, sew the ends in at the end of a row.

If you do find yourself having to sew within the knitted item, first pull the yarn through to the wrong side. Then sew it in working first in one direction, then back in the opposite direction.

SEWING UP – GRAFTING

Grafting can be used to invisibly sew two edges together. Grafting creates a knit stitch, and can be worked on finished (cast-on/cast-off) edges or on live stitches. Items that are grafted together look as if they had been knitted as one piece. In other words, they are (almost) seamless.

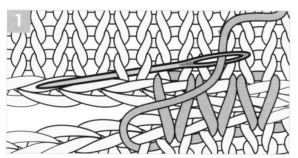

Grafting finished edges together: Work from right to left. Insert the needle from behind into the middle of the lower first stitch. Guide the needle under the two stitch bars of the stitch above the upper part. Insert the needle from the top into the middle of the first lower stitch, then to the front from the middle of the next stitch on the left. Take up the stitch bars of the stitch above, and continue in this fashion to the left edge.

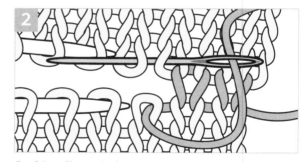

Grafting live stitches together: Guide the needle alternately through the bottom and top of two neighbouring stitches by inserting the needle through the top of the one on the right, and through the bottom of the one to the left of it. Work your way from right to left.

ABBREVIATIONS

dec – decrease/decreases

dpn – double pointed needle

inc – increase/increases

k – knit

k2tog – knit 2 stitches together

kfb – knit into the front and back of one stitch

p – purl

psso – pass slipped stitch over

sl – slip stitch

st(s) – stitch(es)

YO – yarn over

NEEDLE AND HOOK SIZES

metric size	US needle size	US hook size
2.5mm	1 or 2	B or C
4.0mm	6	G
6.0mm	10	J
7.0mm	10½ or 11	K or L
8.0mm	11	L
9.0mm	13	N

UK TO US TERMS

UK term	US term
tension	gauge
stocking stitch	stockinette
cast off	bind off
double crochet	single crochet

PROJECTS

EVERYDAY

INTRODUCTION

It is important for our wellbeing that we consciously organise everyday life away from our commitments; that we pause and take stock, create time for ourselves and our loved ones, enjoy nature and find relaxation there. Nature gives us so much that we value.

The first warm rays of the sun in spring; a sunset in summer; the rustling of autumn leaves; the first snow; trees blowing in the breeze; the sound of raindrops against a windowpane; the chirping of birds; the silence of the forest – nature in everyday life is something wonderful. We can recharge our batteries here, rest after stressful and hectic moments, pause and take stock, relax. Whenever I can, I try to take time and consciously focus on myself and my surroundings and let my thoughts just wander. We like spending time outdoors, working in the garden, cycling down to the lake or taking the dog for a walk. That's why I designed an airy, maritime-style basic striped top in pure organic cotton for hot summer days. For cool rainy days, there's a hard-wearing, warm cowl made of recycled T-shirt yarn that can easily cope with stormy walks with the dog. For shopping, swimming and everyday use, I designed a backpack for which I reused a piece of leather from furniture shop samples. For everything to stay in its place in the backpack, I knitted a little minimalist bag for all the bits and bobs of everyday life.

BASIC TOP

Skills: Beginner, very easy

This basic top knits up easily and very quickly. It consists of two pieces, front and back, knitted in stocking stitch and then simply sewn together up the sides and at the shoulders. The shirt is slightly oversized in style and short enough to be worn tucked-in with high-waist trousers or a skirt. The stripes create a loose, casual look that I love for summer. It's perfect for enjoying the sunset barefoot in a meadow.

SIZES S, M, L

Materials
- Lana Grossa Linea Pura Organico (100% organic cotton, 50g (90m/98yds)): Ecru (006) - 5 balls, and Black (017) - 1 ball
- Label (if desired)

Needles
Circular knitting needle 4.0mm | 60cm long
Wool needle

Stitch patterns
Stocking stitch in rows: Work right-side rows in knit stitch, wrong-side rows in purl stitch.
Rib pattern in rows: Knit 1, purl 1 in turn.

Check the tension
Size 4.0mm needle in stocking stitch: 20 sts and 26 rows = 10 x 10cm (4 x 4in)

Front

Cast on 92 sts.
Rows 1-8: With Ecru work in rib pattern.
Rows 9-16: With Ecru work in stocking stitch.
Rows 17-18: With Black work in stocking stitch.
Rows 19-98: Repeat rows 9-18 8 more times.
Rows 99-114: With Ecru work in stocking stitch.
Row 115: Loosely cast off all sts. The front measures approx. 45 x 46cm (17½ x 18in).
Work the back in the same way.
Spray both pieces with water, smooth them flat and leave to dry.

Finishing off

Place both pieces with the top cast-off edges together on a table and use the wool needle to graft the shoulder seams together (see Knitting Techniques). Work as follows: sew up the first shoulder seam over 25 sts and secure the yarn. Leave a neckline of 42 sts in width, then sew up the second shoulder seam over 25 sts.

Then sew up the side seams. Start at the cast-on edge at the bottom and sew up the sides with the wool needle. Finish at row 68 on both pieces to make the armholes.

Sew in the ends. Steam lightly and sew on the label if desired.

CARE

Follow the manufacturer's washing instructions, shape the garment while still damp and leave to dry.

VARIANTS

In this version for beginners, the armholes were left as the rows they were knitted in. If you like, you can pick up the edge stitches with double-pointed needles in the same size and add some ribbing.

The top can also be made in other sizes:
For size M cast on 102 sts and knit to 50cm (19½in) in length (128 rows).
Start the first black stripe at row 23.
For size L cast on 112 sts and knit to 55cm (21½in) in length (141 rows).
Start the first black stripe at row 29.

The number of stripes remains the same, but are started later in the garment and finish sooner, i.e. the knitted areas in Ecru will be longer at the waistband and at the shoulder/chest stripe. Please allow an additional 100g of yarn for these sizes.

LITTLE CASE

Skills: Beginner, very easy

A little case for pens or to keep in your bag for your phone, charger, cosmetics or a first aid kit – these are always a good idea for an everyday bag! This particular one is made in moments, and a great way to use up leftover yarn.

DIMENSIONS: 10 X 18 CM (4 X 7 IN)

Note: All dimensions above are approximate

Materials
- We Are Knitters The Tape (100% recycled cotton, 250g (120m/131yds)): Beige - 50g
- Alternatively, home-made T-shirt yarn (see Make Your Own T-Shirt Yarn) or scraps of similar cotton yarn: approx. 50g
- Zip, 16cm long
- Label (if desired)

Needles
Double-pointed needles 7.0mm
Wool needle

Stitch patterns
Stocking stitch in rounds: Work all rounds in knit stitch.

Check the tension
Size 7.0mm needle in stocking stitch: 12 sts and 17 rows = 10 x 10cm (4 x 4in)

INSTRUCTIONS

Cast on 40 sts and divide evenly across the needles: 10 sts / needle. Join to work in the round.
Rows 1-18: Work in stocking stitch.
Last round: Cast off loosely.

Finishing off
Sew in the ends. Smooth the case flat and gently steam. Then sew on the label.

Fold the case flat with wrong sides together and sew along the bottom edge. Sew in the zip at the top either by hand or on a sewing machine. Alternatively, use Velcro. Then sew up the open side seam.

BACKPACK

Skills: Slightly advanced skills

The backpack is another favourite project in this book. A collection of leather samples from a discontinued furniture collection that my husband brought home for me had just the right size, and that's how the backpack got its leather flap. I love reusing and continuing to use things, and otherwise the leather would have beenthrown away. But it doesn't matter if you can't get hold of any leather. I explain how to knit the flap in the instructions.

DIMENSIONS: 30 X 33 CM (12 X 13 IN)

Note: All dimensions above are approximate

Materials
- We Are Knitters The Tape (100% recycled cotton, 250g (120m/131yds)): Beige - 300g
- Cord or leather strip: approx. 60cm
- Leather: 22 x 28cm (e.g. furniture sample, scraps from a saddler, orthopaedic specialist or old leather garment)
- Hole punch

Needles
Circular knitting needle 8.0mm | 60cm long
Double-pointed needles 8.0mm
Crochet hook 8.0mm
Wool needle

Stitch patterns
Stocking stitch in rounds: Work all rounds in knit stitches.
Stocking stitch in rows: Work right-side rows in knit stitch, wrong-side rows in purl stitch.
Garter stitch in rows: Work all rows in knit stitch.

Check the tension
Size 8.0mm needle in stocking stitch: 10 sts and 15 rows = 10 x 10cm (4 x 4in)

INSTRUCTIONS

Pouch

Cast on 60 sts with the circular knitting needle and join to work in the round.
Rounds 1-42: Work in stocking stitch.
Round 43: * YO, sl1, k1, psso, k3 *, repeat from * to * 11 more times
Rounds 44-46: Work in stocking stitch.
Round 47: Loosely cast off all sts.

Base

To give the backpack stability, a base is worked instead of simply sewing up the cast-on stitches. This is done by taking up the stitches directly from the cast-on round. The stitches in the cast-on round are divided as follows; 10 sts for the side section of the backpack, 20 sts for the front, 10 sts for the second side section, 20 sts for the back.

Turn the backpack inside out and pick up 10 sts of the cast-on round with one of the double-ended needles. This will be one side of the backpack. For easier orientation, use another needle to mark the 10 sts on the opposite side.

The base is knitted in rows in stocking stitch for the whole length of the backpack.

Rows 1-39: Work in stocking stitch.

Row 40: Cast off but do not cut the yarn. Align the base with the cast-on edge of the backpack and using the crochet hook attach with double crochet. Insert the hook through 1 stitch in the bottom flap and 1 stitch in the edge.

Flap

Punch holes at regular intervals in the leather (approx. every 3cm (1in)) and crochet a row of chain stitches with the crochet hook. Choose the desired shape of the flap on the backpack and decide which row to attach it to. Mark the position using a piece of yarn or pins. Crochet the flap to the marked row.

Alternatively knit flap:

Cast on 22 sts.

Rows 1-45: Work in stocking stitch.

Row 46: Cast off.

Secure the flap to the middle of the back of the backpack using a wool needle or crochet hook.

Straps

The straps are knitted in rows to the desired length. Use a tape measure to check the recommended length of 60cm (23½in) from casting on to ensure it suits you and is comfortable.

Otherwise cast on to the desired length.

Cast on 60 sts on the circular knitting needle.

Rows 1-6: Work in garter stitch.

Row 7: Cast off loosely.

Work the second strap in the same way.

Finishing off

Sew on the straps and thread the cord or leather strips through the loops you made. Sew in all the ends.

CARE

Wash by hand (because of the leather), then pull into shape with your hands and leave to dry. Put some rolled-up hand towels inside the backpack to help it keeps its shape while drying.

VARIANTS

There are lots of options for extending or changing the design of the backpack.

You could knit, sew or crochet the flap instead of making it out of leather. You could also omit it entirely and make it as a drawstring bag instead.

You could repurpose old belts or strips of fabric or leather and sew them on instead of knitting the straps.

Putting leather on the bottom of the backpack will also protect it against dirt and moisture.

EASY PEASY COWL

The Easy Peasy Cowl is a quick project for rainy days and for beginners. The rib pattern is a treat to work and doesn't require too much concentration, which means this is also a good item to make while watching a film or listening to a good audio book without lots of counting. Knitted as a round, it is great for wearing on cooler days with a jumper with a slightly lower neckline, and it won't add bulk worn under a jacket. Turned over once, the collar nestles against you snugly and securely, which instantly makes it one of my favourites for rainy and windy walks.

DIMENSIONS: ONESIZE

Materials
- We Are Knitters The Tape (100% recycled cotton, 250g (120m/131yds)): Grey - 250g

Needles
Circular knitting needle 9.0mm | 60cm long
Wool needle

Stitch patterns
Rib pattern in rounds: Knit 1, purl 1 in turn.

Check the tension
Rib pattern using a 9.0mm needle: 10 sts and 15 rows = 10 x 10cm (4 x 4in)

INSTRUCTIONS
Cast on 60 sts and join to work in the round.
Rounds 1-45: Work in rib pattern.
Round 46: Cast off loosely in pattern. Sew in the ends.

CARE
Follow the manufacturer's instructions for washing. Shape gently while still damp and leave to dry.

KITCHEN

INTRODUCTION

Whether shopping, storage, cleaning or decorating, in the kitchen itself and with anything involving this room, so much can be sustainable. This chapter will give you some ideas for it.

If you've been reading epipa for a while you'll know that we've been living without a dishwasher for years. In the beginning, it was actually only meant to be a little experiment. One balmy evening when we were enjoying a cosy glass of wine on the patio contemplating the garden, my husband said that surely we could wash up by hand in the future. And, picking up the idea and running with it, he said that if our current dishwasher were ever to give up the ghost, perhaps we wouldn't rush out and buy a new one. My initial reaction was to choke on my wine – after all, there are five of us in the family, we love cooking and do so with enthusiasm, and often have guests over. But amused nonetheless, I agreed to the idea, little knowing that 'were ever to' would become the reality just a few weeks later, when our dishwasher did indeed give up the ghost. A year and many dishwater chats later, the experiment had become the reality.

And that is why we need countless tea towels in our kitchen. I particularly like to use ones I have knitted myself.

A tablecloth with a stain that refused to budge, and not having enough place mats in the house resulted in me tearing the fabric into strips and using them to knit place mats.

I like using place mats on the table, firstly because the tabletop is very sensitive to heat – my husband made the table himself and spent many hours and evenings painstakingly covering it in shellac. And secondly, especially when it's cold or particularly unpleasant outside, I like to have coasters and place mats that look nice and add a feeling of warmth.

But the kitchen isn't the only place where you can change things. Every year, up to 10,000 plastic bags are used every day in Germany – that's over 5 billion a year! And often they are only used for the short distance from the shop to home. When I picture this number of carrier bags in a pile in one place, I start to feel quite peculiar, which is why the mesh shopping bags are among my favourite projects in this book.

KITCHEN TOWEL

Skills: Beginner, very easy

Ever since our 'experiment', tea towels have played a key role in our daily kitchen life. I have lots of lovely cotton towels that I like to decorate in the winter months with little embroideries, as well as knitted kitchen towels. More robust and rustic than the tea towels, they have a charm of their very own. They give me a feeling of comfort and well-being, and I love their airy, casual presence in the room. And when the need arises, they can also double as a place mat or potholder.

DIMENSIONS: SMALL 28 X 38 CM (11 X 15 IN)

Note: All dimensions above are approximate

Materials
- Lana Grossa Linea Pura Organico (100% organic cotton, 50g (90m/98yds)): Ecru (006) - 2 balls, and Black (014) - 1 ball or a remnant
- Label (if desired)

Needles
Circular knitting needle 4.0mm| 40cm long
Wool needle

Stitch patterns
Garter stitch in rows: Work all rows in knit stitch.

Check the tension
Size 4.0mm needle in garter stitch: 18 sts and 36 rows = 10 x 10cm (4 x 4in)

INSTRUCTIONS

Cast on 50 sts.

Rows 1-14: With Ecru work in garter stitch.

Rows 15-20: With Black work in garter stitch.

Rows 21-26: With Ecru work in garter stitch.

Rows 27-30: With Black work in garter stitch.

Rows 31-134: With Ecru work in garter stitch.

Last row: Cast off loosely.

Finishing off

Sew in the ends. Smooth the towel flat and steam gently. Sew on the label if desired.

CARE

Although this is pure cotton, which is really quite tough, knitted kitchen towels do need to be treated a little more gently than standard woven ones. Machine wash in a mild detergent at 40 degrees, then gently shape while still damp and dry flat. Then you'll be able to enjoy them for a long time to come.

VARIANTS

These instructions are for a towel in size S. If you'd like your towel to be bigger and wider, simply cast on more stitches: 60 stitches for size M, for instance, and 70 stitches for size L. You can make the towel as long as you like. It should always be a rectangle.

MESH SHOPPING BAG

Skills: Advanced beginner

Once you have internalised the pattern, knitting the bags is easy and won't take long. You can even make them bigger or smaller to suit your purpose and be sure that your purchases will arrive home safely. Due to the mesh structure, the bags will hold almost twice the volume. So you can shop with ease and avoid unnecessary waste. We've tested this several times now, and even I was amazed by how much these home-made bags can cope with and carry. For me, knitting bags has become a lovely project for after work or the weekends, and they make lovely gifts.

DIMENSIONS: SMALL 12 X 18 CM (4½ X 7 IN)
MEDIUM 18 X 24.5 CM (7 X 9½ IN)
LARGE 28 X 32 CM (11 X 12½ IN)

Note: All dimensions above are approximate

Material
- Lana Grossa Linea Pura Organico (100% organic cotton, 50g (90m/98yds)): Ecru (006) - 4 balls
- Cotton cord, 5mm thick: For size S 50cm (20in), for size M 70cm (28in), for size L 100cm (40in)

Needles
Circular knitting needle 4.0mm | 40cm long
Double-pointed needles 4.0mm
Wool needle

Stitch patterns
Stocking stitch in rounds: Work all rounds in knit stitch.
Lacy pattern: Work as described.

Check the tension
Size 4.0mm needle in stocking stitch: 18 sts and 24 rows = 10 x 10cm (4 x 4in)

INSTRUCTIONS

Cast on 40 sts and join to work in the round.

Round 1: Work in knit stitch.

Round 2: * YO, sl1, k1, psso *, repeat from * to * to the end of the round.

Rounds 3-42: Repeat rounds 1 and 2 in turn.

Rounds 43-48: Work in stocking stitch.

Round 49: * YO, sl1, k1, psso *, repeat from * to * to the end of the round.

Rounds 50-55: Work in stocking stitch.

Last round: Cast off loosely.

Finishing off

Lie the bag down flat and sew the bottom (cast-on edge) closed. Sew in the ends. Stretch the bag to open up the lacy pattern, then steam gently and leave to dry.

Thread the cotton cord through round 49. If this is difficult, skip every second loop.

CARE

Follow the manufacturer's instructions. Shape while still damp and dry flat.

VARIANTS

The instructions are for the small mesh bag in size S. In my example, I have cast on 60 stitches for size M and knitted to a length of 24.5cm (9½in).

For size L, I cast on 90 stitches and knitted to a length of 32cm (12½in).

Once you have internalised the pattern, you can knit bags in any size you like. Remember, though, that there should always be an even number of stitches. You can make the bag as long as you like.

HANGING
ORGANISER BASKET

Skills: Advanced beginner

With this basket, I don't know where to begin. It looks good in almost every room in our house. It's perfect for storing keys, hats, gloves in the entrance area and cloakroom; it will hold onions, garlic, ginger or apples in the larder, and keeps guest towels and bathroom utensils neat and tidy in the bathroom. The ring is firmly knitted onto the basket, which means it is absolutely safe to hang up. It's a good idea to knit a few of them, and then enjoy your new, charmingly styled way of keeping the house tidy.

DIMENSIONS: 22 X 20 CM (8 ½ X 8 IN)

Note: All dimensions above are approximate

Materials
- We Are Knitters The Tape (100% recycled cotton, 250g (120m/131yds)): Beige - 150g
- Alternatively, home-made T-shirt yarn (see Make Your Own T-Shirt Yarn): approx. 150g
- Curtain ring

Needles
Double-pointed needles 7.0mm
Crochet hook 7.0mm
Wool needle

Stitch patterns
Rib pattern in rounds: Knit 1, purl 1 in turn.
Stocking stitch in rounds: Work all rounds in knit stitch.
Lacy pattern: Work as described.

Check the tension
Size 7.0mm needle in stocking stitch: 12 sts and 17 rows = 10 x 10cm (4 x 4in)

INSTRUCTIONS

Cast on 40 sts as follows:

Needle 1: Cast on 10 sts.

Needle 2: Cast on 2 sts, crochet 6 sts into the curtain ring and thread onto the needle, cast on 2 sts onto the needle (fig. 1).

Needles 3-4: Cast on 10 sts on each needle (fig. 2). Join to work in the round.

Rounds 1-4: Work in rib pattern.

Round 5: * YO, sl1, k1, psso *, repeat from * to *.

Round 6: Work in stocking stitch.

Rounds 7-20: Repeat rows 5 and 6.

Rounds 21-25: Work in stocking stitch.

Rounds 26-28: k2tog until only 5 sts are left on the needle.

Finishing off

Fasten off, leaving a tail of about 20cm (8in). Using the wool needle thread the tail through the remaining stitches, tighten the yarn to close the opening, and secure the yarn end safely.

CARE

Hand wash because of the wooden ring. Shape while damp. If desired, roll up a hand towel and place upright in the basket while it dries.

VARIANTS

The instructions are for a small basket. To make a bigger one, simply cast on more stitches. 50 stitches for size M, for instance, and 60 stitches for size L. You can make the basket as long as you like.

Thinking ahead to what you are planning to use it for, though, do remember that the mesh pattern is very stretchy and will expand in length and width depending on the weight or volume of the contents. And remember, too, that depending on the weight (e.g. apples or potatoes), the hanging hook needs to be very firmly attached to the wall.

PLACE MATS

The fabric, torn into strips, and uncomplicated rustic pattern will make the prepared table look much cosier and friendlier. These place mats were cast on and knitted in the width. This results in a very pretty horizontally striped pattern. It's important that you knit it very loosely. The fabric strips are not stretchy, like wool is, and so won't slip over the needle as easily if your knitting is too tight.

DIMENSIONS: SMALL 35 X 26 CM (14 X 10 IN)
MEDIUM 40 X 30 CM (15½ X 12 IN)
LARGE 45 X 35 CM (17½ X 14 IN)

Note: All dimensions above are approximate depending on the material in this example

Materials
- Home-made cotton tape yarn (see Make Your Own Cotton Tape Yarn, this version is made from an old tablecloth): approx. 125g (depending on the fabric thickness) per place mat
- Alternatively, We Are Knitters The Tape (100% recycled cotton, 250g (120m/131yds)): 125g per place mat
- Label (if desired)

Needles
Circular knitting needle 7.0mm | 40cm long
Wool needle

Stitch patterns
Garter stitch in rows: Work all rows in knit stitch.

Check the tension
Size 7.0mm needle in garter stitch: 10 sts and 22 rows = 10 x 10cm (4 x 4in)

INSTRUCTIONS

Cast on 35 sts.
Rows 1-55: Work in garter stitch.
Last row: Cast off loosely.

Finishing off

Sew in the ends. Smooth the place mat flat and steam gently. Add a decorative label if desired.

CARE

Wash as for the original fabric. Shape while damp and leave to dry.

VARIANTS

The place mats are knitted in size S, and will fit under cake plates and soup bowls on a small table.

For bigger mats:
Size M: Cast on 40 stitches and knit 63 rows for 40 x 30cm (15½ x 12in).
Size L: Cast on 45 stitches and knit 75 rows for 45 x 35cm (17½ x 14in).

*"LOOK DEEP INTO
NATURE, AND THEN
YOU WILL UNDERSTAND
EVERYTHING BETTER."*

Albert Einstein

KITCHEN BASKETS

Skills: Beginner, very easy

I love to use baskets to store all kinds of things around the house. Including in the kitchen for rolled up tea towels, place mats or food that we want to use up in the course of a week. Ginger, garlic, onions, brussels sprouts, but also bread and rolls look pretty and appealing stored in these baskets.

DIMENSIONS: 10 X 15 CM (4 X 6 IN)

Note: All dimensions above are approximate

Materials
- We Are Knitters The Tape (100% recycled cotton, 250g (120m/131yds)): Grey - 50g
- Alternatively, home-made T-shirt yarn (see Make Your Own T-Shirt Yarn): approx 50g
- If desired, leather tab and 1 stud or label

Needles
Double-pointed needles 8.0mm
Wool needle

Stitch patterns
Garter stitch in rounds: Alternate rounds: work round 1 in knit stitches, round 2 in purl stitches.
Stocking stitch in rounds: Work all rounds in knit stitch.

Check the tension
Size 8.0mm needle in stocking stitch: 12 sts and 17 rows = 10 x 10cm (4 x 4in)

INSTRUCTIONS
Cast on 40 sts and divide evenly over the set of needles: 10 sts / needle, join to work in the round.
Rounds 1-4: Work in garter stitch.
Rounds 5-24: Work in stocking stitch.

Rounds 25-27: K2tog until only 5 sts are left on the needle.

Finishing off
Fasten off, leaving a tail of about 20cm (8in). Using the wool needle thread the tail through the remaining stitches, tighten the yarn to close the opening, and secure the yarn end safely. Turn over the top edge, and if desired secure the leather tab as decoration. Studs are available on the internet or from haberdashers. Please follow the manufacturer's instructions.

CARE
Follow the care instructions on the band and leave to dry. Shape while damp. If desired, roll up a hand towel and place in the basket so it keeps its shape while it dries.
If you are using the leather tab on the basket, please follow the care instructions for the leather.

VARIANTS
These instructions are for a small basket. To make bigger ones, simply cast on more stitches. 60 stitches for size M, for instance, and 70 stitches for size L. You can make the basket as long as you like.

To ensure it remains stable, make it in a cube shape rather than having it too tall.

DISH SPONGE

These little cotton sponges are ideal for light dirt and gentle on delicate surfaces such as glass or stainless steel. For slightly heavier dirt, you can also substitute sisal or jute for the cotton and use the results as little scourers. I love these little sponges because, unlike dishcloths, they tolerate a certain amount of rubbing. They are also ideal for using up yarn remnants, and are quick to knit and replace when old ones have come to the end of their lifetimes.

DIMENSIONS: DIAMETER 8 CM (3 IN)

Note: All dimensions above are approximate

Materials
- Lana Grossa Linea Pura Organico (100% organic cotton, 50g (90m/98yds)): Ecru (006) - 1 ball
- Alternatively, remnants of cotton yarns in a similar thickness: approx 50g

Needles
2 double-pointed needles 4.0mm or circular knitting needle 4.0mm
Wool needle

Stitch patterns
Garter stitch in rows: Work all rows in knit stitch.

Check the tension
Size 4.0mm needle in garter stitch: 24 sts and 18 rows = 10 x 10cm (4 x 4in)

INSTRUCTIONS

Cast on 25 sts, leaving a 30cm (12in) tail of yarn, as this will be needed later on.

Row 1: Kfb, knit to 2 sts before end, k2tog.

Row 2: K2tog, knit to last st, kfb.

Rows 3-20: Repeat first and second rows 9 more times.

Last row: Cast off loosely leaving a long tail of yarn, and fasten off.

Finishing off

Fold the ends over so they cover the whole straight area and create a rectangle.

Use the wool needle to sew the cast-on and cast-off edges together (fig. 1). Gather one of the open sides together and pull tightly (fig. 2), taking care not to break the yarn! Sew in the end.

Repeat for the other side, but this time insert the needle through the middle of the sponge repeatedly to join the two layers together. Sew in the ends – and you're done.

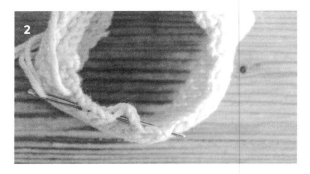

BATHROOM

INTRODUCTION

The bathroom is a haven of relaxation and harmony. It's
somewhere to escape from everyday life for a while, and just
restore the balance between body and soul.

My days are often very busy and active, and so I have
made a habit of regularly taking time out for myself
and treating myself to some self-care. It could be a
rainy weekend day spent in cosy clothing, with a detox
tea and soul food, or just a little time in the evening
when I make myself some tea, listen to relaxing music,
watch a film and put on a home-made face mask.

I try to take some time out for myself once a week
to slow down and pamper myself for a while. A little
time out for body and soul, dedicated just to me and
my well-being. Then it's time for a home spa day. My
daughter often joins me, and we have a lovely mother-
and-daughter session together.

I even enjoy the preparations with pleasure. I light
scented candles, find some relaxing music, make a pot
of detoxing herbal tea or detox water, and if it's cold
and wet outside – well, so much the better! Along with
the detox and soul food, massages and exfoliations are
an essential part of my home spa days.

We all know that a good body scrub boosts the
circulation, removes dead skin, stimulates the skin's
repair mechanism, and is excellent preparation for the
creams or lotions and masks that are to follow. That's
why I have not only designed a massage glove, but a
body scrubby for the back as well.

BODY SCRUBBY
MASSAGE GLOVE

Skills: Beginner, very easy

You can buy countless different variations of a massage glove in shops, made in materials ranging from nylon and polyester to natural products such as hemp or sisal. But as my grandmother would have said, "You can easily make your own!". The little Body ScrubbyMassage Glove doesn't take long to knit and is very easy to make. The cotton cuff makes sure it fits well, while the double strand (one cotton, one sisal) massage surface is wonderful for a body scrub.

DIMENSIONS: 14 X 24 CM (5 ½ X 9 ½ IN)

Note: All dimensions above are approximate

Materials
- Lana Grossa Linea Pura Organico (100% organic cotton, 50g (90m/98yds)): Light Grey (029) - 1 ball
- Alternatively, remnants of cotton yarns in a similar thickness: approx 50g
- Sisal or jute yarn, 3mm (⅛in) diameter: 100m (110yds)

Needles
Double-pointed needles 4.0mm
Double-pointed needles 8.0mm
Wool needle

Stitch patterns
Rib pattern in rounds: Knit 1, purl 1 in turn.
Garter stitch in rounds: Alternate rounds: work round 1 in knit stitch, round 2 in purl stitch.

Check the tension
With an 8.0mm needle and two strands of yarn, one cotton and one sisal or jute, in garter stitch: 22 sts and 24 rows = 10 x 10cm (4 x 4in)

INSTRUCTIONS

Cast on 40 sts in cotton yarn and join to work in the round.

Rounds 1-19: Work in rib pattern.

Round 20: Continue in the rib pattern, working loosely as you'll change to 8.0mm needles in the next round.

Round 21: Change to 8.0mm needle. Add sisal yarn to continue with a double strand, and dec the number of sts in this round: k2tog until only 20 sts remain on the needle.

Rounds 22-38: Work in garter stitch.

Last round: Work dec: k2tog until only 10 sts are left on the needle.

Finishing off

Fasten off, leaving a tail of about 25cm (10in). Using the wool needle thread the tail through the remaining stitches. Tighten the opening and sew in the ends.

CARE

Rinse in clear water after using and dry in a well-ventilated place.

"You have to feel nature."

Alexander von Humboldt

BACK SCRUBBY

Skills: Beginner, very easy

Gentle exfoliation stimulates the blood circulation, it is easier for the body to transport toxins from the cells, the skin feels fresher and revitalised, and is ready to absorb creams and masks for the full effect. So it goes without saying that a sisal body scrubby must be part of the process. I've knitted it with two strands, one of sisal and one of cotton yarn. This gives the right level of exfoliation.

DIMENSIONS: 15 X 50 CM (6 X 19½ IN)

Note: All dimensions above are approximate

Materials
• Lana Grossa Linea Pura Organico (100% organic cotton, 50g (90m/98yds)): Stone (029) - 1 ball
• Alternatively, remnants of cotton yarns in a similar thickness: approx 50g
• Sisal or jute yarn, 3mm (⅛in) diameter: 200m (220yds)
• 2 wooden handles if desired (I used old curtain rings)

Needles
Circular knitting needles 9.0mm
Wool needle

Stitch patterns
Garter stitch in rows: Work all rows in knit stitch.

Check the tension
With a 9.0mm needle and two strands of yarn, one cotton and one sisal or jute, in garter stitch: 22 sts and 24 rows = 10 x 10cm (4 x 4in)

INSTRUCTIONS
Cast on 15 sts with both yarns.
Rows 1-94: Work in garter stitch.
Row 95: Cast off loosely.

Finishing off
Sew in the ends, then sew the handles on to the two ends.

CARE
Rinse in clear water after using and dry in a well-ventilated place.

VARIANTS
If you don't have any wooden handles, simply crochet or knit a length of cord and sew on.

SMALL BATHMAT

Skills: Beginner, very easy

The subtle and uncomplicated pattern of this little bathmat looks just as at home in a romantic, rustic bathroom as it does in a clear, modern one. It is very easy to knit with no counting, and can easily be made in a weekend. I made it with recycled yarn from T-shirt production. Because of its small size, though, it can also be made from home-made T-shirt yarn or torn cotton strips.

DIMENSIONS: 38 X 54 CM (15 X 21½ IN)

Note: All dimensions above are approximate

Materials
- We Are Knitters The Tape (100% recycled cotton, 250g (120m/131yds)): Beige - 500g
- Alternatively, home-made T-shirt yarn, or home-made cotton tape yarn (see Make Your Own Cotton Tape Yarn): approx. 500g
- Label (if desired)

Needles
Circular knitting needle 7.0mm | 60cm long
Wool needle

Stitch patterns
Stocking stitch in rows: Work right-side rows in knit stitch, wrong-side rows in purl stitch.

Check the tension
Size 7.0mm needle in stocking stitch: 12 sts and 17 rows = 10 x 10cm (4 x 4in)

INSTRUCTIONS

Cast on 41 sts.

Row 1: Knit all sts.

Row 2: K1, p1 in turn

Rows 3-5: Repeat first and second rows once more, then work row 1 once.

Row 6: Work stitches 1-5 as edge stitch (k1, p1 in turn); purl stitches 6-26, work stitches 37-41 as edge stitches.

Row 7: Knit all sts.

Rows 8-80: Repeat rows 6 and 7.

Rows 81-85: Work as rows 1–5.

Row 86: Loosely cast off all sts.

Finishing off

Sew in the ends. Smooth flat and gently dampen the mat and leave to dry. Add a label or leather tab if desired.

CARE

Follow the manufacturer's instructions. With recycled yarns such as T-shirt yarn or cotton strips, handle the mat like the original material.

VARIANTS

The instructions are for a bathmat in size S. For a bigger one or even a rug, simply cast on more stitches, e.g. 61 stitches for size M, and 81 stitches for size L. Always work the first and last 5 stitches in a row as edge stitches. Choose the length to suit you. The result should always be a balanced rectangle.

HAIRBAND

My spa hairband keeps fine, short hairs off my face and helps to make sure that a mask or scrub only goes where you want it to. It is also useful when applying make-up or removing it in the evening. The hairband is knitted in stocking stitch on double-pointed needles, then folded in half and sewn together at the end. This means it will keep you nice and warm, and can also be worn outside the bathroom.

DIMENSIONS: 7 CM (3 IN) WIDE, UNSTRETCHED 45 CM (17½ IN) CIRCUMFERENCE OR AS DESIRED

Note: All dimensions above are approximate

Materials
• Lana Grossa Linea Pura Organico (100% organic cotton, 50g (90m/98yds)): Light Grey (029) - 1 ball

Needles
Double-pointed needles 4.0mm
Wool needle

Stitch patterns
Stocking stitch in rounds: Work all rounds in knit stitch.

Check the tension
Size 4.0mm needle in stocking stitch: 18 sts and 24 rows = 10 x 10cm (4 x 4in)

INSTRUCTIONS

Cast on 24 sts, leaving a 30cm (12in) tail and divide them evenly across the needles (6 sts per needle). Join to work in the round.

Rounds 1-80: Work in stocking stitch.

Fasten off and using the wool needle thread the tail through the remaining stitches, tighten the yarn to close the opening.

Finishing off

Thread the cast-on tail onto the working yarn and pass it through the cast-on stitches. Carefully close the opening, taking care not to break the yarn. Place the two ends of the hairband together and sew up with the wool needle. Sew in the ends, but do not fasten off.

Wind the remaining length of yarn around the seam until you have made an attractive "knot". Sew in the end and trim.

CARE

Follow the instructions on the band. Shape while damp and leave to dry.

VARIANTS

The hairband should fit firmly and not too loosely around your hairline so it keeps all the fine hairs safely out of your face. The instructions are for a snug fit, which is why my hairband is about 45cm long. If in doubt, place the hairband around your head as you would wear it before casting off at the end. If the cast-on edge and the stitches on the needles touch with just a gentle pull, then you have the right length. Otherwise knit a few more rounds to adjust the length.

FACIAL PADS
FOR THE HOME SPA

Skills: Experienced beginner

These little pads in pure linen are double knitted with two different surfaces. The coarse side in garter stitch is ideal for gentle exfoliation of the delicate skin of the face. Applied in massaging movements, the smooth, structured side in stocking stitch will remove all traces of make-up and everyday stress from the face. I also like using these pads as warm compresses soaked in a decoction of marigold and then placed on my eyes.

DIMENSIONS: 8 X 8 CM (3 X 3 IN)

Note: All dimensions above are approximate

Materials
• Lana Grossa Linea Pura Solo Lino (80% recycled linen, 20% linen, 50g (120m/131yds)): Grège (002) - 1 ball

Needles
2 double-pointed needles 2.5mm
Crochet hook 2.5mm
Wool needle

Stitch patterns
Stocking stitch in rows: Work right-side rows in knit stitch, wrong-side rows in purl stitch.
Garter stitch in rows: Work all rows in knit stitch.
Textured pattern: The pattern is created using stitches lower down, which are staggered into every 6th row, i.e., instead of knitting the current stitch, insert the needle in the stitch four rows below the current stitch, knit this stitch, and drop the stitch above it in the current row off the needle. Then knit the next 3 stitches in the current row. The textured pattern will appear after the twelfth row.

Check the tension
Size 2.5mm needle in stocking stitch: 25 sts and 36 rows = 10 x 10cm (4 x 4in)

INSTRUCTIONS

Textured side

Cast on 19 sts.
Row 1: Purl all sts.
Row 2: Knit all sts.
Row 3: Purl all sts.
Row 4: Knit all sts.
Row 5: Purl all sts.
Row 6: k3, * insert needle in st 4 rows below and knit this st (drop the 3 sts above), k3 *. Repeat from * to * to the end of the row.
Rows 7-11: Work as rows 1-5.
Row 12: k1, * insert needle in st 4 rows below and knit this st (drop the 3 sts above), k3 *. Repeat from * to * to the last 2 sts in the row. Then insert needle in the st 4 rows below and knit this st (drop the 3 sts above), k1.
Rows 13-24: Work as rows 1-12.
Rows 25-30: Work as rows 1-6.
Row 31: Cast off loosely. Sew in the ends.

Exfoliating side

Cast on 19 sts.
Rows 1-30: Work in garter stitch.
Row 31: Cast off loosely. Sew in the ends.

Finishing off

Place the piece in garter stitch on the table, and put the textured piece on top of it with the right side facing up. Crochet around both pieces in double crochet inserting the hook in the edge st of the top and bottom pieces together. Sew in the ends.

CARE

Machine wash in a mild detergent at 40 degrees, then gently shape while still damp and dry flat. By doing this you'll be able to enjoy these pads for a long time to come.

Traces of make-up, tea or herbal decoctions may stain the pads. If you don't like the idea of this, then make them in a dark colour.

SCRUNCHIE

Skills: Beginner, very easy

You can make all sorts of lovely little things out of leftover yarn. However, apart from coffee cosies and coasters, there is also another way of knitting lovely things from scraps of wool. Little hair ties and charming scrunchies are quick and easy to make yourself with thin elastic band.

DIMENSIONS: DIAMETER 12 CM (4 ½ IN)

Note: All dimensions above are approximate

Materials
• Scraps of yarn, e.g. Lana Grossa Linea Pura Organico (100% organic cotton, 50g (90m/98yds)): Ecru (006)
• Elastic 1–1.5cm (½in) wide: 22cm (8½in)

Needles
Circular knitting needle 4.0mm | 40cm long
Wool needle

Stitch patterns
Stocking stitch in rounds: Work all rounds in knit stitch.

Check the tension
Size 4.0mm needle in stocking stitch: 20 sts and 28 rows = 10 x 10cm (4 x 4in)

INSTRUCTIONS
Cast on 85 sts and join to work in the round.
Rounds 1-20: Work in stocking stitch.
Round 21: Cast off loosely. Fasten off, leaving a length of approx. 60cm (23½in).

Finishing off
Cut a 22cm (8½in) length of elastic and sew the ends together. Turn the scrunchie inside out, place the elastic on the inside, and sew the working yarn alternately through the stitches from the cast-on and cast-off rows. Take up the stitches of the plain knit side that are visible loosely, and work from bottom to top Gently pull the working yarn from time to time to make room for the elastic. Do not pull too tightly, because you will have to loosen the yarn again later on.

When you have taken up all the stitches, pull the scrunchie with the elastic to its full length and loosen the yarn to the maximum length of the elastic. When you have done this and adjusted the seam to the flexibility of the elastic, secure the end and sew in.

CARE
Wash in accordance with the manufacturer's instructions.

VARIATIONS
You could also make the scrunchie in rib pattern or garter stitch, for instance.

LIVING ROOM

INTRODUCTION

The living room is where family life happens. It's where
we cuddle, relax and spend time together.

I always like to use old duvet covers, discarded or from a flea market, and breathe new life into them. I use them to make clothing, cushion covers and quilts, and for my first book I tore them into strips and used them to weave a nursery rug, just like my grandmother once did. For this book, I wound the strips into balls of yarn and knitted a table runner from them. Its rustic look and the fine marl from the patterned fabric conjure up a cosy atmosphere, especially on cool rainy days.

The living room is generally a place of comfort and relaxation. It's where we read, listen to audio books together, play board games and use quiet moments for meditation.

Meditation means 'finding the core' in the sense of 'deliberating, contemplating, reflecting', and is a spiritual exercise that is used in many religions and cultures to calm the mind and gather one's thoughts. Above all, the aim is to find inner peace: to return mentally to the here and now. To consciously slow down everyday life with its numerous duties and tasks, and to reboot. My husband and I try to meditate for 10–15 minutes every day and allow our thoughts to calm and rest. Meditation cushions can be a great help with this. Find out how to knit them in this section.

*"Meditation puts us
in touch with what
holds the world
together at its core."*

Johann Wolfgang von Goethe

TABLE RUNNER

Skills: Beginner, very easy

For this book, I simply ripped the remnants of a duvet cover into strips and knitted a small table runner from them. Its rustic appearance provides so much comfort, especially in the cold season. I cast on the runner in the width and knitted until I ran out of yarn. This resulted in a lovely lengthways pattern. It's important that you knit it very loosely. The fabric strips are not stretchy, like wool is, so they won't slip over the needle as easily.

DIMENSIONS: SMALL 40 X 55 CM (15 ½ X 21 ½ IN)

Note: All dimensions above are approximate depending on the material in this example

Materials
- Home-made cotton tape yarn (see Make Your Own Cotton Tape Yarn, made here from half an old duvet cover in a woven fabric)
- Label (if desired)

Needles
Circular knitting needle 8.0mm | 60cm long
Wool needle

Stitch patterns
Garter stitch in rows: Work all rows in knit stitch.

Check the tension
Size 8.0mm needle in garter stitch: 8 sts and 12 rows = 10 x 10cm (4 x 4in)

INSTRUCTIONS
Cast on 45 sts and work in garter stitch until you get to the end of the cotton yarn or the runner is the size you want it to be. Cast off loosely.

Finishing off
Sew in the ends. Gently steam the runner. Sew on the label if desired.

MEDITATION CUSHION

Skills: Beginner

Our little cushions make sure my family and I are sitting comfortably when we meditate. They relieve the pelvis and spine, and help us to relax more easily.

DIMENSIONS: DIAMETER 30 CM (12 IN)

Note: All dimensions above are approximate

Materials
- We Are Knitters The Tape (100% recycled cotton, 250g (120m/131yds)): Beige - 150g
- Alternatively, home-made T-shirt yarn (see Make Your Own T-Shirt Yarn): approx. 150g
- Spelt husk cushion insert, 30cm (12in) diameter
- Alternatively, fabric remnants, old towels, T-shirts etc. for the filling

Needles
Circular knitting needle 8.0mm | 60cm long
Wool needle

Stitch patterns
Rib pattern in rounds: Knit 1, purl 1 in turn.

Check the tension
Rib pattern using a 8.0mm needle: 10 sts and 15 rows = 10 x 10cm (4 x 4in)

INSTRUCTIONS

Cast on 60 sts and join to work in the round.

Rounds 1-40: Work in rib pattern.

Last round: Take up all the sts on the wool needle and close the opening with the working yarn. Sew in the end and trim.

Finishing off

Cut a new piece of yarn approx. 50cm (19½in) long. Thread the wool needle and take up the stitches in the cast-on row, leaving a piece hanging down loosely on both sides. Carefully draw the opening together (take care not to tear the yarn), but do not close completely.

Insert the cushion pad or filling and pull the opening. Tie the length of yarn in a bow to close the cushion cover.

CARE

Untie the bow, open the cover and remove the insert. Wash in accordance with the manufacturer's instructions. If made from fabric remnants, wash as usual for these materials. Wash loose fabric remnants in a cotton bag or pillowcase. If you like, you can make your own insert using the fabric remnants on a sewing machine.

Follow the manufacturer's instructions for the cover. Shape gently while still damp and leave to dry.

PATCHWORK MAT

Skills: Beginner

This mat is one of my favourite pieces in this book because it is so incredibly versatile and can be knitted from almost any materials. In this example, a strip of the patchwork mat measures approx. 55 x 20cm (21½ x 8in), and was knitted entirely from a single type of yarn, The Tape. According to We Are Knitters, this yarn is made from leftover materials from T-shirt production. I loved using it for many of the projects in this book because it is so robust. The mat is just as suitable for making from your own T-shirt yarn or from cotton strips. The individual pieces don't all have to be the same length. You can create very nice patterns of strips in different lengths and widths, because not all home-made yarns are the same length. Simply knit the individual pieces in their various widths and lengths, or incorporate the individual yarns in strips. If using knitted pieces of different lengths, two or three together should always measure 55cm (21½in) in total. There are almost no limits to what you can do.

DIMENSIONS: 110 X 55 CM (43½ X 21½)

Note: All dimensions above are approximate

Materials
• We Are Knitters The Tape (100% organic cotton, 250g (120m/131yds)): Grey - 750g
• Alternatively, home-made T-shirt yarn (see Make Your Own T-Shirt Yarn): approx. 750g
• Yarn remnants in white

Needles
Circular knitting needle 8.0mm | 60cm long
Crochet hook 8.0mm
Wool needle

Stitch patterns
Stocking stitch in rows: Work right-side rows in knit stitch, wrong-side rows in purl stitch.
Garter stitch in rows: Work all rows in knit stitch.

Check the tension
Size 8.0mm needle in stocking stitch: 10 sts and 15 rows = 10 x 10cm (4 x 4in)

INSTRUCTIONS FOR ONE STRIP MEASURING 20 X 55 CM (8 X 21½ IN)

Cast on 20 sts.

Rows 1-2: Work in garter stitch.

Rows 3-80: Work in stocking stitch.

Rows 81-83: Work in garter stitch.

Last row: Cast off loosely. Sew in the ends.

Finishing off

For the mat shown in this example, knit four more strips as instructed above.

Then dampen all the pieces and leave to dry. Line up the long sides of the strips (fig. 1) and double crochet the edges together in a contrasting yarn (fig. 2). This will create a raised seam that adds texture.

You can alternatively sew the pieces together with the wool needle.

CARE

Follow the manufacturer's washing instructions, shape the garment while still damp and leave to dry.

VARIATIONS

These instructions for using up fabric remnants can also be used to make patchwork quilts or plaids as well.

ABOUT THE AUTHOR

Epipa, which is also the name of the eponymous blog **www.epipa.de**, lives with her husband, three children, two cats, one dog and lots of hens in their house in the country. She loves anything and everything you can make or do yourself, and has been sharing this passion with her readers for over 10 years now on her blog, Ravelry, Etsy and Instagram @_epipa_. She has already published several books in Germany, which have become much-loved classics.

THANKS

Thank you from the bottom of my heart to everyone who supported me with my fourth book.

My family for your patience when things got tight and I had a deadline to meet, and for your support over the many months that I spent hidden away in my office working on the manuscript. Thank you for unconditionally and enthusiastically putting up with all my ideas and experiments on any subject. I love your open-minded manner, your input and your interest in new ideas – and in particular your ability to think outside the box and blaze new trails. It's just great being with you!

My husband – thank you for your support, for having my back, and for doing the important things in the background so that I am able to work. Thank you for creating this wonderful home for us and for deciding 20 years ago to be as self-sufficient as possible and use the sustainable building methods that we are still benefiting from today. As a team, we are unbeatable.

My eldest son – thank you for your help with the shoots. I love your eye for motifs and perspectives. I love being able to share my passion for photography with you, and I love talking shop with you! Even though we come from two different worlds photographically, we always manage to find common ground and are able to achieve unbelievable synergy effects.

My daughter – thank you for once again so patiently being my model for what is now my fourth book, you old hand. I always love the shoots with you. You have a wonderful talent for making pictures uncomplicated and exciting, and you bring a lightness to every single one of them. I love your charm and your humour, and I'm looking forward to starting our next project.

My younger son – thank you for your way of showing me things from a different perspective. You shake up our world, and that's refreshing. You're the coolest little guy I know, and I love being silly with you. Thank you for every new angle you give me.

Thanks to my **parents and grandparents** for teaching me respect for life, nature and her resources when the term sustainability was still years from being fashionable. I thank you, because it is your values that I live and pass on to my children. Thank you for your love and support.

Thanks to **my mother-in-law** for being our sheet anchor for this, our fourth book, happily running 'Granny's taxi service', cooking, ironing and babysitting for the grandchildren when the going got tough. I can tell you that things would have been pretty challenging without you many times!

A huge thank-you to **our friends**, who once again had to give up on me for many months because I had once again completely hidden myself away in my workroom. I am so happy that you are always there – and come and rescue me from time to time.

And last, but by no means least, thanks always to **my ever-loyal community**, who have supported epipa for so long. Thank you for your perpetual feedback that supports me, motivates me and keeps spurring me on. Thank you for your loyalty and enthusiasm. It's brilliant fun to write for you. You are the best, and you inspire me.

Many thanks also to **Lana Grossa** and **We Are Knitters**, who provided me with my favourite yarns for this book that I have been using for my projects for over 15 years now.

A very big thank-you also to **Carmen Düll of Namensbänder.de**, who supported my work on this book with the fabulous SnapPap vegan leather labels that added that certain extra something to so many of the projects.

SOURCES

Namensbaender.de

Supplier of the SnapPap labels seen in the book, vegan leather, made from cellulose and latex. SnapPap is made in Germany. According to the manufacturer, it is environmentally friendly and is obtained from sustainably managed forests. namensbänder.de prints SnapPap labels with individual texts or your own logo.

Lana-Grossa.de

Manufacturer of the Organico and Solo Lino yarns used in this book. Organico is made from certified organic cotton, while Solo Lino contains 80 percent recycled linen.

Weareknitters.de

Manufacturer of The Tape yarn used in this book, which is made from recycled cotton.

Finkhof.de

The sheep farming cooperative Finkhof offers sustainably dyed wool from German sheep and source addresses of German sheep farms that are committed to the issues of new wool from controlled organic husbandry, environmental protection and animal welfare.

Bioland.de

Offers a purchasing guide for wool and wool products from Germany and source addresses.

Schmusewolle.de

Mail order retailer for dyed yarns and dyes. According to its company philosophy, Schmusewolle attaches the greatest importance to loving husbandry and animal-friendly shearing, and guarantees that its wool is 100% mulesing-free.

Myboshi.net

Ready-made dyeing kits, individual or as creative sets with six pots of dye and the wool of choice.

DONATIONS

Some organisations such as children's, premature and angel baby charities will happily accept donations to bring happiness to others or reduce pain and suffering. You will find countless addresses on the internet.

Terms such as 'knitting for preemies', 'knitting for angel babies', 'knitting for homeless' or 'donate knitting' will result in numerous addresses of organisations that will be pleased to accept your knitted donations or organise creative meetings.

INDEX

A DAVID AND CHARLES BOOK
© 2020 Edition Michael Fischer GmbH, Donnersbergstrasse.
7, 86859 Igling

This translation of EINFACH NACHHALTIG STRICKEN first
published in Germany by Edition
Michael Fischer GmbH in 2020 is published by arrangement
with Silke Bruenink Agency,
Munich, Germany.

David and Charles is an imprint of David and Charles, Ltd
Suite A, Tourism House, Pynes Hill, Exeter, EX2 5WS

First published in the UK and USA in 2021

Text and Designs © Epipa 2020
Design: © 2020 Edition Michael Fischer from the book
'Einfach nachhaltig stricken'.

Sascia Strohhammer has asserted her right to be identified
as author of this work in accordance with the Copyright,
Designs and Patents Act, 1988.

The author and publisher have made every effort to ensure
that all the instructions in the book are accurate and safe,
and therefore cannot accept liability for any resulting injury,
damage or loss to persons or property, however it may arise.

Names of manufacturers and product ranges are provided
for the information of readers, with no intention to infringe
copyright or trademarks.

A catalogue record for this book is available from the
British Library.

ISBN-13: 9781446308813 paperback
ISBN-13: 9781446380925 EPUB

This book has been printed on paper from approved
suppliers and made from pulp from sustainable sources.

Printed in the UK by Buxton Press for: David and Charles, Ltd
Suite A, Tourism House, Pynes Hill, Exeter, EX2 5WS

10 9 8 7 6 5 4 3 2 1

David and Charles publishes high-quality books on a wide
range of subjects. For more information visit
www.davidandcharles.com.

Layout of the digital edition of this book may vary depending
on reader hardware and display settings.

CREDITS
Cover design: Anna-Maria Köperl
Project management: Anja Sommerfeld, Saskia Reusch
Editing: Ute Wielandt
Layout: Luca Feigs
Typesetting: Yvonne Witzan
Photos: © Sascia Strohhammer (with the exception of the
following); © Lana Grossa (p.16), © Pascuali (p.16), © Rico
Design (p.18), © We Are Knitters (p. 18, 19), © ggh yarn
(p. 19), © Lieblingsfarben @myboshi (p. 27)
Graphics: © Barisikina/Shutterstock (leaves), © Strejman
(care symbols), © Global Organic Textile Standards (p.21), ©
OEKO-TEX® (p. 21), ISBN 978-3-96093-589-6

© Edition Michael Fischer GmbH, 2020